Get a G.R.I.P.

By

Richard Leo Hunt, EdD

First Edition ©2021
Trade Paperback Edition

Published in the United States. Printed and bound in the United States of America.

No part of this book may be reproduced or transmitted in any form or by any means without written permission of the author.

Sale of this book without a front cover may be unauthorized. If this book is coverless, it may have been reported to the author as "unsold or destroyed" and neither the author nor the publisher may have received payment for it.

Get A Grip is a work of non-fiction. Any resemblance to actual persons, living or dead, events, or locales is entirely coincidental unless specifically cited by the author.

The author respects trademarks and copyrighted material mentioned in this book by introducing such registered items in italics or with proper capitalization.

Cover Art Design:
Farah Evers Designs
FarahEversDesigns.com

Interior Book Design: Farah Evers

Illustrations: Farah Evers

Author Photograph by J. Lamar Creative

Editing: Farah Evers

Editing/Proof Reading: Derek Odom

Copyright © 2021 by Richard Leo Hunt

All rights reserved.

Table of Contents

Introduction	- 1 -
Chapter 1: Gratitude	- 3 -
Chapter 2: Responsibility	- 17 -
Self-Efficacy	- 23 -
Cognitive Biases	- 32 -
Poor Decision Making	- 37 -
Chapter 3: Improvement	- 54 -
Goal Setting	- 69 -
Emotional Intelligence	- 86 -
Chapter 4: Positivity	- 92 -
Self-Regulation	- 98 -
Emotion Regulation	- 101 -
Five Steps to Overcome Negative Thoughts	- 108 -
Resilience	- 113 -
Bouncing Back	- 119 -
Summary	- 128 -

INTRODUCTION

Much of this book is based on material that is readily available for anyone. However, a significant portion is from my own personal experiences and reflections. I am presenting it to you from my perspective, with my own twist, stories, and research findings. I hope my interpretation and explanations of these concepts resonate with you and my stories help inspire you in some way to get a GRIP on your life. All the poems were written by me and I hope you enjoy them as well!

One of my all-time favorite quotes is from the movie, The Matrix, where Morpheus is talking to Neo at the end of the rooftop rescue scene:

"Neo, sooner or later you're going to realize just as I did that there's a difference between knowing the path and walking the path."

Thankfully, I came to realize that simply knowing what characteristics I want to incorporate and strengthen in no way guarantees anything other than being able to talk about them. Learning how to harness and employ them has taken time and effort through self-reflection, self-awareness, critical thinking, and extensive research. The characteristics and qualities that I continuously practice and incorporate into my own life are Gratitude, Responsibility, Improvement, and Positivity. If you ever feel like life is slipping through your fingers, then get a GRIP.

"I breathe in the beauty of the world around me and exhale gratitude."

CHAPTER 1: GRATITUDE

There will be times when we experience events, circumstances, relationships, etc. that are adverse and require a serious consideration of the potential negative consequences, exploration of risks, and realistic analysis of the situation. However, it is important to neither dwell nor ruminate on the negative aspects for an extended time. If I find myself floundering in worry, I quickly find something for which to be thankful and express my gratitude mentally, verbally, or in writing. A state of gratitude sets me more at ease and helps me focus more on outcomes that I desire. Gratitude brings a good feeling that proliferates more of the same way of thinking and behavior. With gratitude as a foundation, I can generally reframe any circumstance, event, or relationship in a positive way.

Feelings can get you. They can hit hard or come on softly. Either way, they are trying to tell us something. Sometimes, I wonder if what I feel is correct for the situation or if maybe I am just not interpreting them correctly. Let's face it, they can be quite complex. Some people state that our thoughts can become "hijacked" by the emotional part of our brains because it processes information faster than our rational part. Others state that most emotions are reactions to physical stimuli and our brains then create feelings. But, at other times emotions and feelings are triggered by what we think, like what we tell ourselves or visualize. Geez! My head is spinning! However, I tend to believe that in general, feelings are important and deserve our attention. We should allow for some thoughtful analysis. Just try not to overthink because it is easy to get so caught up in them that we lose touch with reality. So, take a deep breath and allow yourself to feel some gratitude for this very moment.

Gratitude can be thought of as a life orientation for noticing and appreciating (realizing the full worth or implications of something) the positive aspects of life. We can experience gratitude for what is inside of us and what we already have or from what is outside of us such as other people, nature, or a higher power. Gratitude is positively correlated with improved mood, energy, health, life satisfaction, and overall well-being. Research abounds with data supporting how gratitude journals, speaking gratitude, or even just thinking about it lowers stress, cortisol levels, inflammation markers, toxic emotions, and depression. It can improve relationships and can be used in conjunction with psychotherapy to improve overall mental health. Gratitude helps me to become more grounded and balanced when things seem to be slipping out of control.

There are two things for which I strive: staying grounded and maintaining balance. My challenge is that I think those things sound incredibly boring. So, what to do? Well, I choose to accept myself as the type of person that craves growth (which means that change is inevitable) even if it means disrupting the status quo, while at the same time realizing that aiming to stay grounded and balanced keeps me from going off the deep end. Not that the deep end is necessarily bad, but it can be a long way down and you had better be ready for some rough water. In any case, I feel the most grounded and balanced when I'm in a state of gratitude.

When I think of balance, I imagine optimum situations like "evenly distributed" or "steady" although sometimes it is about keeping myself from falling – in more ways than one. In any case, trying to find and maintain balance can be a struggle. It requires constant mindfulness of internal shifts and external forces so that we may counteract them in some way to continuously maintain balance. It can feel like we are constantly striving to achieve balance rather than attaining it.

As a personal example, if I am constantly taking action and outwardly expressing myself, then I'm not slowing down to go inside and reflect. I am neglecting the moment and not appreciating it. I am not allowing myself to feel good about what I have now, what I'm achieving, and I may forget to express my gratitude. At the same time, I can get so caught up in feeling good in the present that I am not focusing on my goals and I am not taking the necessary steps to achieve them. I feel like I have become stagnant. I may be failing to take some necessary action because I am avoiding the possible anxiety or stress that can accompany tasks and timelines because I am so caught up in just feeling good right now.

> Take heed of the moment
> For the sun will surely set
> and let not your worries
> lead you to regret.
> Take the reigns of your spirit
> and lead yourself through will
> for you have a purpose
> and a destiny to fulfill.
> Be thankful for the chance
> to do something now
> for the sun will surely rise
> no matter the how.

I must admit, an overly structured environment makes me feel anxious and constrained; however, I also do not like the feeling of not having some degree of control over certain aspects of my surroundings. As an example, it drives me crazy when I cannot find something I am looking for! And I know that is on me and it is my responsibility. Then I start thinking about changing something in my life to get closer to that balance that I seek. Oh, so many gurus and experts ready to tell us to change our thoughts and feelings and behaviors, but what is often missing is the "how." If change is forced upon us, and I mean literally forced, then we are generally good at adapting. It may take longer for some than others and that is okay, but just be cognizant of potential consequences, especially if there is a choice to resist. But, if a change is suggested, maybe subtly or covertly, then we may wonder if it is a form of control or manipulation and be resistant. Does it make us better in general or is it simply to meet someone else's needs and goes against our values in some way? I believe we must make it our own in a way that is right for us. We must have a solid "why" to fuel our motivation, create some kind of a plan, and be able to measure our progress according to the phases of that plan that are always subject to refinement. Be grateful for any opportunity to be better, celebrate the successes, learn from the setbacks, be kind to yourself and others, and never let anyone make you feel like you deserve less than what you want.

I have read and listened to countless books by Brian Tracy. I love how he breaks down subjects and shares his life experiences. One particular topic that has stuck with me is Brian's explanation of the five levels of personality. The first level is our values. Have you ever really thought about what you value in life? And what can be even harder is ranking them. The best way I have found to understand my values is to think about things for which I am most grateful. What we value determines our beliefs about ourselves and the world around us. What we believe then determines our expectations. As an example, if you are grateful for your health, then you place a high value on it. You will probably also appreciate all the incredible systems that make up the body, how they function, and how every cell in your body is working in harmony to keep you well and alive. This will in turn affect your beliefs. You might believe in taking good care of yourself. You will believe that it is important to optimize your health through eating habits, exercise, good sleep, etc. This will lead you to have expectations of being healthy. The next level is your attitude.

I tend to think of an attitude as an outward expression of our thoughts, feelings, and overall demeanor about something. In our example, you will have a positive attitude about your health and how you are affecting it. It will be expressed verbally and most importantly, in your actions, which is the fifth level. If you value your health, believe in affecting it positively, expect to have good health, and have a positive mental attitude toward your health, then your behavior will support all of this. You will take action to ensure your health is as good as it can be. You will take care of yourself.

This is how I believe having and expressing gratitude for something attracts more of it into our lives. What do I mean by attract? At a minimum, there is something called the Baader-Meinhof phenomenon which supports the whole idea of attracting things into our lives. Basically, when a concept or thing is in the front of our mind for whatever reason, we tend to pay attention to our environment for that which matches or supports the concept or thing. The phenomenon is synonymous with a cognitive bias called frequency illusion. We are selecting that which we pay attention to and through confirmation bias, we convince ourselves that it is meaningful and supportive. We want more of it and this drives our behavior. So, why not use it to our advantage? By focusing on that for which we are grateful, we place a value on it, and this affects our beliefs, expectations, attitude, and eventually, our behavior, which leads to taking the necessary actions to bring it into our reality. We attract more of it into our lives. Now, I believe it goes much deeper than that, but I hope you can see this practical explanation.

I believe it is important to have a goal, believe in it, visualize it, and feel as though it has already been achieved. When we do this, we are planting the seed, watering it, caring for it, and allowing it to germinate. This intention activates the processes already within ourselves that draw upon our experiences, knowledge, observations, intuition, and environment to generate and create ideas in support of the goal. Even with the awareness of risks and possible consequences, we must take action in the face of the fear of failure (among other fears) in order to start the chain of events necessary to cause the goal to come to fruition. From this, we have created an expectation. We expect something to be created. We are desiring a given outcome and I believe that the forces of the universe will conspire to make it a reality for us so long as our intentions are driven with positive energy.

Nonetheless, we must be careful that we do not become attached to a specific outcome. If we have strong expectations and we are attached to an outcome, we can be "let down" if things do not turn out just the way we planned. This can feel like something is not working out right and the process has let us down. However, an outcome that is different from the original idealized goal is oftentimes a very good thing. We may get what we need (love, happiness, peace, etc.) instead of what we thought we needed (a new relationship, a bigger car, more money, etc.). But, if we allow ourselves to feel let down, then we are failing to show gratitude for that which we have accomplished which probably would never have happened had we not had the original goal and taken the necessary action in the first place.

Sometimes, it is good to just take a deep breath and be thankful for the moment. When there is a whirlwind of tumultuous activity around you and chaos runs abound, you can bring order to your mind, body, and soul by taking a deep breath and thinking of something for which you are grateful. It may be something simple that only lasts for a moment, but that moment can cause an immediate shift in your perception and the effects can last a long time. Talk show mogul Oprah Winfrey is quoted as saying: "Focusing on one thing that you're grateful for increases the energy of gratitude and raises the joy inside yourself." Country music singer Willie Nelson is another that has professed the importance of gratitude in his life: "When I started counting my blessings, my whole life turned around."

I have always been intrigued by the "moment." Like, what is a moment? Is it the shortest interval of time that one can perceive? Is the moment different for each individual? I love the idea of trying to focus on and capture a moment with the shortest amount of time while simultaneously trying to perceive it for as long as possible. In other words, I am trying to minimize the amount of time for a given moment while trying to expand and maximize the amount of time that I use to perceive it. Think about this: As we let a moment approach the absolute smallest perceptible amount of time, then the number of moments we live approaches infinity. Sometimes, at any given moment, I am overwhelmed with gratitude to the point of getting goosebumps all over which is then followed by a deep breath that is exhilarating. Time seems to slow down to the point where that particular moment has in some way expanded or dilated in my consciousness. I feel connected, energized, and powerful. Then, I want to hold onto that feeling, but the very thought of wanting to hold on causes the feeling to vacate. It's in those moments that I feel as though I get a glimpse into the infinite. At the same time, I realize that to truly experience the ever-fleeting moment to its fullest potential and the euphoria that accompanies the deep connection to it, I must let go. I am seeking balance.

For me, the balance lies in the art of having goals, making plans, and taking action, while staying grounded is about beholding the moment as much as I can and expressing gratitude for the infinitely wonderful things in my life. So, while striving for balance may seem like a struggle, my advice is to embrace it by being grounded. Be open to the wondrous possibilities that come your way. Be thankful for the opportunities and experiences. Show gratitude for the breath you just took.

I am thankful in every possible way for the wonderful things that are happening today. As I think the thoughts of positive expectations,

I am sending out harmonious vibrations that resonate with those of like kind and attract into my life those of like mind. They are drawn in with a magnetic appeal and mirror the essence of what I feel. When opportunity knocks I will open the door and for each new friend, the gratitude will pour.

I know I will prosper in every possible way for I receive what I have given every single day.

CHAPTER 2: RESPONSIBILITY

Does taking responsibility for your actions make you think of blame? Does it conjure up feelings of guilt, fear, and shame? From interacting with others and my personal experience, I believe this happens often. It is so easy to avoid these negative thoughts and feelings by blaming other people, circumstances, and a myriad of other possibilities for the things that were well within our control for an unwanted outcome. When we do that, we give up power. By taking responsibility for our behavior, feelings, and ultimately the very thoughts that drive them, we empower ourselves. It allows us to reflect on what we could have done differently and then put a plan in place to do better. Trust me, I understand that there are external factors, circumstances, people, and other things that we can't control and which affect our situations. But don't give them power over what you can control. Instead, own it and take that power back into your own hands.

If I blame other people or circumstances for any negative outcome in my life, then I am giving power to something outside of myself and I feel less in control. By taking responsibility for our actions, behavior, and attitude, we feel more empowered. We can focus on the causes within ourselves by reflecting on our actions, behavior, attitude, and thoughts. We can then go to work on correcting the factors over which we have control instead of blaming those which we have little or none. This is a very empowering way of engaging life, but not always an easy task. It takes a strong desire and a strong effort.

During basic training in the army, I remember quite vividly standing there watching the other members of my squad throw a grappling hook up through a window and climb it successfully. I was a nervous wreck.

My palms were sweaty, my heart rate was up, and I wasn't sure if I could do this. I joined the Army for several reasons: I needed to grow up, take on responsibility, and be in an environment where I was practically forced to complete something. I knew this about myself and I am thankful that I did. While my service was relatively mild compared to others, my experiences, and the challenges that I faced were life-changing for me. Some of the challenges would evoke a fear of failure and criticism that I kept to myself. Anytime I was tasked with something that required upper body strength, I was terrified. My legs were strong, but my arms and upper body were weak relative to my body size. One day, as part of an urban obstacle course, we were learning how to throw a grappling hook through a window, climb up the wall, and then make our way into a window. I watched as most of my other squad members shuffled up the wall, and very few struggled much. I was so worried that I wouldn't make it that I wanted to hide. I was scared that I would look weak in front of everyone and they would make fun of me. I did not believe that I could do it.

When it was my turn, the drill sergeant stuck his head out of the window (which was approximately 25 feet off the ground) and shouted at me to throw the grappling hook through the window. I successfully threw it through the window and was happy that I got that much right, at least. I gripped the rope tightly and placed my foot on the vertical wall. As I lifted the other foot, I slipped, fell forward, and bounced off the wall. I took a deep breath and tried it again. This time, I put one foot up, then the other, and started walking up the wall. About halfway up, my forearms were burning, and I stopped. I looked up and saw my drill sergeant's head and his huge hat sticking out of the window. He was yelling at me to keep going. I looked down and saw my fellow squad members yelling at me to keep going. I took a couple more steps and was only a few feet from the window. I stopped again and froze up. My arms were shaking. The drill sergeant started yelling at me to just go back down.

I looked up and decided that one way or another, I was going to make it into that window. At that moment, even though my arms were strained to the max, I was so close that I finally believed I could make it the rest of the way. This was a turning point in what I was thinking and what I believed, which in turn directed my actions and effort. I knew that if I could just get my foot in the window, that I could use my leg strength to pull myself up the rest of the way. I held on tightly, took a couple more steps, and as my foot made it into the window, I was able to pull myself up and through the window. This was a challenge that changed my life.

I find it amazing how the mind and body will respond to what we tell ourselves and what we believe. Sometimes, what we tell ourselves leads to a belief, and other times a belief is what determines what we tell ourselves. If they contradict, we can experience a form of cognitive dissonance that can negatively affect our attitude, decisions, and behavior. However, when what we tell ourselves and what we believe are aligned, we can overcome great obstacles in our lives. But we will never get to that point unless we take responsibility. By taking responsibility, we set ourselves up to employ personal resources to control an outcome. If we believe that we can't, then we find ways to shed responsibility to alleviate an inner struggle. In general, people with high self-efficacy tend to set more challenging goals because they believe in their abilities to perform the necessary tasks and activities, which influences their expectations for a desired outcome.

Self-Efficacy

Some time ago, I was waiting to audition for a role and I suddenly realized that instead of being nervous I was calm, confident, and full of gratitude for the opportunity. I still had a feeling of excitement, but it was not dampened with anxiety. Now, do not get me wrong, I realize how tough it is to get a role and callbacks can be few and far between. However, what's liberating is that I can allow myself to feel good at the moment without getting too caught up in the possible (and most probable) outcome. What is most important is showing up; it is paying our dues through experience, mistakes, setbacks, and wrestling with our insecurities and self-limiting beliefs so that we keep moving forward. Just keep going and all those fears and anxieties will step aside to allow a sense of confidence to take over because you've "been there and done that." It is not arrogance and it is not cockiness, but it's a steady calm backed by the forces of perseverance and determination grounded in a state of gratitude.

If you lack self-confidence in a certain area of your life that is important to you, then it is okay to try and dig in to understand the causes. However, try not to spend too much time there because you can start to question so much and second-guess yourself to the point of just giving up and accepting your current state. My suggestion is to begin doing something that will slowly increase your self-confidence. Yes, your mind will resist, you will come up with excuses, and those self-limiting beliefs will induce a wide range of feelings but being aware of these things will help you to not get bogged down. Listen, accept that it is going to take time, and get started as soon as possible. Imagine your future self-expressing gratitude to the person you are today for having the courage to go for it.

I appreciate experiences so much. Regardless of the turnout, I am very grateful to have an opportunity to learn. Take on that experience and see how it feels, how you think, and how you behave. And I believe it is okay to lose yourself a little along the way. Not so much that you lose your mind, body, or soul, but allow yourself to change. Take what you learn from the experience and assimilate it. Incorporate that which serves you into your worldview and add those elements to your character. Change can be challenging, difficult, and even painful at times, but why not try? You will come out stronger, wiser, and have a widened perspective on life. And no matter what, try your best to be thankful along the way, but most of all, be grateful for what you have learned in the end.

One of my favorite psychologists is Albert Bandura. He is known for his pioneering work in social cognitive theory and self-efficacy. Self-efficacy is defined by Bandura as "people's beliefs about their capabilities to produce designated levels of performance that exercise influence over events that affect their lives. Self-efficacy beliefs determine how we feel, think, motivate ourselves, and behave." Regarding expectations: "An outcome expectation is defined as a person's estimate that a given behavior will lead to certain outcomes. An efficacy expectation is a conviction that one can successfully execute the behavior required to produce the outcomes." This difference is important because we may believe that certain actions can lead to a given outcome, but if we have doubts about our abilities to perform those actions, then we are not influenced to take the necessary steps. Why is this important? Because we need to believe in ourselves! We need to believe in our abilities to do that which needs to be done to achieve our goal. If your belief is not strong, then do what it takes to make it strong. So, how can we do that?

Bandura suggests four ways to better believe in ourselves and our abilities: thinking about past-related success, learning and replicating others, positive suggestions made by others, and controlling our emotions. It makes sense that past successes, especially those related to the current situation, positively affect our belief that we can accomplish more. What about past failures? Generally, failures lead to a reduction in self-efficacy; however, this is dependent on how we perceive and define the failure. As an example, we may gain competence in performing tasks, especially doing something over and over again, but we may fail to accomplish the desired outcome. If we attribute the failure more to external factors, such as the environment or unexpected changes, rather than us not performing well enough, then self-efficacy may not be negatively affected. Remember, there is a difference between efficacy and outcome expectations. This can lead to trying again, especially if we truly believe that what we are doing will lead us to goal achievement.

When we observe other people achieving their goals and note what they did to achieve them, which may be more about overcoming adversity through determination and perseverance, then this observation can generate similar expectations within us. In other words, if someone else can do it, then so can we! We just need to follow their example and model their behaviors, such as effort and perseverance. Has anyone ever suggested that you could accomplish your goal? It sure feels good and it can motivate us to get started and stay with it. It can help us to overcome adversity and setbacks by remembering that someone else believes in our abilities to perform tasks and persevere.

But what if we are fearful of failing in the face of adversity? Responding to stressful circumstances with fear can debilitate our performance and lead to elevated states of anxiety. Fear can feed off itself by way of conjuring up fear-provoking thoughts and images of poor performance; however, if we can regulate our emotions through strategies such as seeking help or just talking to a friend, it can lessen the fear response, thereby reducing its effects. Sometimes, we judge ourselves poorly after a setback, but how we respond to this judgment matters. It is oftentimes natural for us to have an immediate reaction of self-doubt, but what matters most is how quickly recover.

Here is where it is important to take full responsibility for the beliefs in our capabilities to perform and our commitment to achieving our goals. If we fail, it is okay to take our share of the responsibility to learn from our mistakes so that we can apply that learning toward the next attempt or goal. There is a big difference between attributing a failure to a lack of ability compared to a lack of effort. If we succeed, it is also okay to take our share of the responsibility so that we can feel good about it and allow our self-efficacy to increase along with our ability to achieve a certain outcome.

There is also a big difference between performance goals which are more approval-oriented and mastery goals that tend to be more learning-oriented. When we set performance goals (I need to find a way to achieve this target by this date), we tend to attribute failure to our lack of ability, and this may lead to giving up. Setting mastery goals (I am going to put forth a great effort and learn this to the best of my ability) will most likely cause us to attribute failure to a lack of effort and will lead us to try again with even more determination. This leads to another important distinction: fixed versus growth mindset. People who have a fixed mindset are more likely to have performance goals and lower resilience while those with a growth mindset are more mastery-oriented and have higher resilience. This is significant. See how this is lining up?

Goal Type	Orientation	Attribution	Mindset	Resilience
Performance	Approval	Ability	Fixed	Lower
Mastery	Learning	Effort	Growth	Higher

On one side we can see a correlation between having a performance goal, needing approval, relying on ability, and having a fixed mindset. On the other, we see the correlation between having a mastery goal, learning, effort, and growth. So, go at it with a mindset of "I can learn how to do this, I will try as many times as I need, and I will seek support when I need it" instead of, "If I can't get this right, then I guess I'm not cut out for it or just not smart enough so I might as well give up." So what's the point?

It is certain that we will make decisions regarding important aspects of our lives and that we will lack all the data necessary to make a risk-free decision with a guarantee of success in every instance. Mistakes will be made, setbacks will be incurred, and failure will be known to even the most well-intentioned. When we experience a failure, we may undergo a period of disappointment, depression, and grief. We will question our identity, lose self-esteem, and become disillusioned. Our feelings and thoughts about ourselves can spiral downward to the point of apathy and listlessness. But, through the process of self-observation, our thoughts, feelings, and behaviors can be monitored and assessed in how they affect our motivation. With a sense of willpower, we can transition to a state of resilience. Resilience is about adapting to the failure and gaining emotional stability, balanced optimism, and coherence through self-regulation, which lead to behaviors involving goal setting and planning for success. Then, we must act purposely and manage our energy toward goal achievement. Our effort along with self-efficacy can lead to a sense of value, positive expectations, and determination. As motivation increases to the point of action, a sense of agency dominates when we feel in control of our destiny.

Cognitive Biases

What if we fail despite good intentions? A failure can result from errors in judgment and decision-making. These errors are sometimes rooted in systematic ways of thinking that vary, stemming from logical and rational thought processes. Such systematic deviations in thought are referred to as cognitive biases which are narrow ways of thinking about options, objectives, and our future. These biases can unknowingly lead to a tendency to be in favor of or against something or someone, especially when we are emotionally invested. The implication is that we are generally unaware of our cognitive biases and that we have good intentions. We can experience failure due to poor decision-making that is ultimately rooted in one or more cognitive biases. Here are a few to be aware of:

1. Confirmation bias: A tendency to gravitate toward information that confirms what people already believe and

downplay information that disconfirms their beliefs.
2. Fundamental attribution errors: People tend to attribute success to their skills and insights while downplaying luck and external factors.
3. Normalization of deviance: This is the tendency over time to accept anomalies —particularly risky ones — as normal and downgrade the importance of near misses.
4. Outcome bias: Successful outcomes can cause too much focus on the results instead of the complex processes that created them.
5. Overconfidence bias: Successes can cause people to believe that they are better decision-makers than they are.

We may be oblivious of our cognitive biases and our inability to think rationally and clearly as a result of the biases. Before decisions are made, positive and negative outcomes should be considered and risk assessed. Assessing risk includes considering the probability of the outcome and consequences of the outcome — both positive and negative. An honest assessment of both possible outcomes should be considered: the reward of a good outcome and the severity of a bad outcome. In other words, what are the possible consequences? What are the positive and negative effects of the possible consequences?

As an example, if the gas light comes on indicating a low fuel level while traveling to a destination by car, it may depend on the situation as to whether or not we stop for fuel. Certain questions may be considered in our minds before a decision is made. Is the amount of fuel left in the tank known or estimated? How much farther is it to the destination? What is the estimated distance that could be traveled based on the known or estimated fuel left in the tank? This first set of questions is an attempt to assess the risk of running out of fuel before reaching the destination. If the risk is high, more questions will be asked. If a stop for fuel is made, is it likely that the arrival time will be after the scheduled appointment? What are the consequences of being late? If the negative consequences of being late are high, then we may downplay or ignore questions about the consequences of running out of fuel.

There is an interplay between our thoughts and emotions that can lead to a bias and result in a poor decision. Additionally, the absence of all relevant data and information needed for systematic decision-making can lead to a certain type of bias called a heuristic, especially under pressure and time constraints. It is a shortcut to making a decision or, sometimes, called a "rule-of-thumb." Decision heuristics are subject to errors and biases but can be highly useful in making decisions. Although errors in judgment and decisions that result from cognitive biases are somewhat predictable, they are not apparent to us or we ignore them because of factors such as time constraints and pressure. Cognitive biases are not the only human element where we mean well and yet still make poor decisions.

Poor Decision Making

Making decisions can be simple or complex; however, the level of complexity of the decision-making process does not necessarily implicate the complexity of the decision to be made. Making a decision is about choosing among alternatives. If there is only one option available, then it is easy, take it or leave it. Even this type of decision can potentially create confusion, frustration, and immobilization.

> If your worries are so heavy
> that each step is full of pain
> and you slowly come to a stop
> as your energy starts to wane,
> then focus on the moment,
> be thankful that you are here
> and in your heart, you will find
> the strength to persevere.

Sometimes, I get stuck on a decision. I just cannot seem to make a timely choice between available options. It can be as simple as what to eat next or more complex, as in such as what to do with my life. But regardless of the type, relative importance, number of options, etc., there seems to be a common theme for me. First, I need to make sure I am clear on the desired outcome or goal. Second, the available options must be vetted against an estimated probability that each choice will lead to the desired conditions or outcome. Third, there are usually multiple factors to be considered for each option and each of the factors needs to be categorically understood and explicitly stated. Finally, these factors need to be prioritized and weighted by importance. Granted, some decisions are fairly easy to make without too much thought, but if I'm ever having trouble or feeling confused, then the aforementioned items are usually what's holding me up. By thinking through these items, I can make my decision faster and feel better about it. Does that guarantee success? No. Does a failure mean it was all fruitless? Once again, no. The key is to learn why the decision was not the best. In other words, why did it not lead to the desired outcome or not without significant obstacles that could have been avoided? Even if the new outcome is accepted, assimilate the information gleaned from a little bit of analysis and use it for the next related decision. You will get better and faster at making good, solid decisions. However, there will still be mistakes.

I love John Maxwell's definition of a system: "A system is a process for predictably achieving a goal based on specific, orderly, repeatable principles and practices." I would make a simple change and state that a system "is a process or set of processes," which better implies the possible complexity of a system. At a high level, a process involves inputs, resources, interrelated procedures, decisions, and outputs. Depending on the process, inputs can be objects such as raw materials and components or more abstract such as data and information. Ideally, inputs are well defined and clear. Inputs initiate some type of action to be taken. These actions involve tasks, practices, or procedures that require resources such as people, time, machines... etc. Then decisions are made that analyze the inputs and transform them into something new. The goal is to acquire an outcome from all of this energy. The outcome or output may become an input for a new process. Imagine a factory that brings in raw materials and parts from all over the world so that people and machines might assemble a vehicle. This vehicle eventually becomes an input into the sales process. An outcome could also be a decision (e.g., yes, you qualify for the loan or no, you were denied the benefit). In a perfect system, the outputs would always come out as designed and perfect in every way. But, as we all know, this rarely happens.

An aspect that is often forgotten is that all systems have some degree of error. There exists variation in the inputs, resources, and how procedures are carried out, all of which contribute to error in the output when compared to some perfect standard. I know of no system which is devoid of all variation and is therefore perfect in every respect. So, if there is variation in the output, how do we know it's still "good?" The output is usually compared to a standard and can be tested by checking or measuring certain characteristics and features. Some variation is allowed and because a difference is expected, an acceptable tolerance is assigned. However, even the test and measurement method have errors and sometimes a good object is determined to be bad and vice versa. An output that is a decision such as yes/no is relative to a truly correct decision and the same type of mistakes can happen (it was a "no" when it should have been a "yes") because of the overwhelming amount of information and data that must be analyzed. The information, data, and method of analysis are all subject to error of some kind.

When it comes to decisions, there can be Type I or Type II errors. In general terms, a Type I error (false positive) is when a decision has been made that something is not good, rejected, deemed too different, or has changed in some significant way compared to a standard or truth when in fact, it has not. A Type II error (false negative) exists when there has been a failure to detect something truly wrong or different. Depending on the circumstances, steps can be taken to reduce the probability of either the Type I or Type II error. When the probability of one type is decreased, the probability of the other type is increased. I will attempt to explain this better with some examples that experience Type I and Type II errors.

When a pharmaceutical company is researching the possibility of a new drug to be introduced to the population for some condition, a lot of testing is required to ensure its efficacy. If a false positive or Type I error occurs, then the research suggests that the drug has the desired effect when it truly does not. If the drug has known harsh side effects and possibly some that are unknown, then this is an undesirable outcome because a significant amount of time and money will be spent in marketing and preparing the drug to be released to the population. The drug would be released to the public with the negative side effects that will be experienced by the users with no real positive effects of helping the condition. It is best to reduce this type of error. When the probability of this type of error is reduced, the probability of a Type II error is increased. For the given scenario, it is better to fail to recognize that the desired effect exists than to incorrectly accept that the drug works when it does not. The cost of negatively affecting people's lives with no benefit for their condition is greater than the missed opportunities of a drug that works.

In a manufacturing environment, it is important to identify parts that vary too far from the standard which is then deemed to be nonconforming. Oftentimes, testing occurs intending to reject bad parts and pass parts deemed acceptable. This ideal situation would ensure that no defective parts make it to the customer. If a false positive or Type I error occurs, then a good part is rejected as though it had an unacceptable level of variation and potential cause defects when in fact it was a good part. When a false negative or Type II error occurs, a part is passed as though it had an acceptable level of variation and conformed to the standard when in fact, the part was unacceptable. A Type II error is an undesirable outcome because the nonconforming part could be passed along to the customer which could lead to a defect and that would be much more costly. When the probability of a Type II error is reduced, the probability of a Type I error is increased. Again, it is better to absorb the cost of some falsely rejected parts than to pass defective parts on to the customer.

Sometimes, a truly innocent person is arrested and found guilty. This is a Type I error. When a truly guilty person is found to be "not guilty" then it is a Type II error. (Notice that innocence is not proven, but instead, there is not enough evidence to find a person guilty.) The American system is purposely designed to avoid Type I errors. Finding an innocent person guilty not only sends the wrong person to prison, but the guilty person is still free. While a Type II error also sets a guilty person free and is not desirable, at least an innocent person does not go to jail.

Think about people in our society that receive financial assistance or free health care. There is a system in place to decide who gets it and who does not. Some people get it that truly do not qualify and other people that truly qualify and need it, won't get it. Remember, when you reduce the probability of one type of error, you increase the probability of the other. Where do you stand? Yes, it is better to have a more accurate system. But, until that happens, you must make a choice. Given that there is variation in the system and inherent error in the decisions, would you (a) rather see fewer people get the assistance that does not qualify while also reducing the number of people getting it that do qualify or (b) accept the fact that there are people who will get the assistance that don't qualify while making sure the maximum number of people get the assistance that does qualify?

In all cases, we want the system to be perfect. It rubs us the wrong way that we must accept these mistakes. And it is annoying that we have to think about which mistake is better and then design the system to be biased in that direction. The best we can hope for is to minimize the variation and improve the overall system so that decisions on both sides are more accurate. But that is not as easy as it sounds. There are numerous factors or inputs (information, data, measurements, etc.) that must be considered, appropriately weighted, and analyzed by people, and software using processes that hopefully provide a good output to aid in a decision. There are going to be mistakes. Accept it.

Another source of mistakes is cognitive biases that are specific to the decision- making process. Below is a list of several cognitive biases and some methods of decision making that carry inherent risks:

1. Satisficing: Choosing the first alternative that meets the minimum requirements or that is considered good enough.

2. Heuristics: A rule of thumb that simplifies complex decisions.

3. Primacy/recency effect: When information discovered early (primacy) or late (recency) influences the decision-maker to a greater degree.

4. Bolstering the alternative: When one alternative is preferred over others even before the information is gathered and then only information that rationalizes the choice (related to confirmation bias).

5. Intuition: A quick evaluation based on experience and knowledge.

6. Incrementalizing: Making small changes successively until one alternative is chosen; referred to as muddling through.

7. The garbage-can method: Problems, solutions, and resources are figuratively thrown into a garbage can, and patterns are explored to find appropriate matches.

These types of decision-making methods carry inherent risks that increase the chances of error and failure. Sometimes, we make debilitating mistakes, and a common reason is having overconfidence in our ability to succeed. So, what can we do to make better decisions?

I will not bore you with the details of a couple of decision-making models that I have researched. The main point of each is to try and make the best decision possible. Below is a diagram that shows a decision-making process:

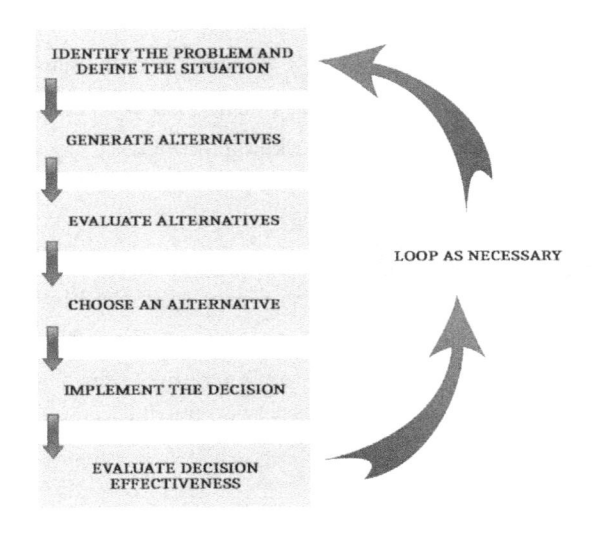

```
IDENTIFY THE PROBLEM AND
DEFINE THE SITUATION
         ↓
GENERATE ALTERNATIVES
         ↓
EVALUATE ALTERNATIVES                LOOP AS NECESSARY
         ↓
CHOOSE AN ALTERNATIVE
         ↓
IMPLEMENT THE DECISION
         ↓
EVALUATE DECISION
EFFECTIVENESS
```

The first and most critical step is to correctly identify the problem. If you are in a perfect world, then all information is known, complete, and the situation is ideal to make an optimum decision. This would require resources and time to gather relevant information in the environment from anyone performance rating anything that might provide relevant information and data. Next, alternatives are generated that are in alignment with the goals and outcomes we want to achieve. The third step is evaluating all the alternatives for feasibility, how well each addresses the problem, and their impacts or consequences.

From this, an alternative is chosen, implemented, and evaluated for effectiveness. Depending on the analysis, the cycle may need to be repeated many times. Frequently, the nature of the problem is obscure, there are uncertainties, unknowns, and a lack of resources to conduct a comprehensive evaluation and analysis. Most likely, we are faced with inadequate information, all possible alternatives are unknown, consequences of alternatives are unpredictable, and it is accepted that finding an optimal alternative is unlikely. My point is this: Make the best decision you can with the information you have, take responsibility for the outcome, learn from it, and always be open to learning and changing.

If we want to grow, then we must accept change. What do you see when you look in the mirror? Do you see yourself how others see you? Or how a voice in your head judges you? Or what about what you want to be? Is it possible to see yourself objectively? I think a lot about authenticity and sometimes I wonder if I can even know for sure if I am being authentic at times. To me, it means that our behavior or what we project out to the world represents our true selves. And what does that mean? Is it when we act impulsively and do not think about it? Must we always feel good about it? What if we want to change?

Some experts assert that we can never change certain aspects of our core personality and that we can only change our behaviors. I believe it comes down to being in alignment with your true values. Just like the most successful organizations tend to make decisions that are aligned with their values, so should we as individuals. Sometimes the decision will not be popular, may be criticized, and even judged as wrong by others, but *you* should feel it was right and feel good about it. Be happy with the person you see in the mirror or make a change because the reflection you see is the person *you* are projecting.

To fully incorporate the growth, we must express it as authentically as we can through our thoughts, feelings, and behaviors. But how do we know if we are being true to ourselves? I tend to pay close attention to my feelings. If I feel a sense of dissonance, then I know something is not aligned with my thoughts and behaviors and I can almost always pinpoint the problem. At that point, I must make a decision. Do I push myself to fully incorporate the change or do I revert to my old ways? It is not always easy, but if you understand your process, then you are better suited to guide yourself to where you want to be. No matter what, take responsibility for yourself, and try your best to enjoy the ride.

You may remember or have heard of Charles Barkley, who played in the NBA from 1984-2000 and is considered one of the greatest NBA players of all time. He was also a controversial sports figure who had a temper. He would get angry at external factors and take his anger out on the court. In 1991, a heckler in the crowd at an NBA game was shouting racist remarks at Barkley.

In the fourth quarter, Barkley saw the heckler once again and attempted to spit on him. Instead, he spit on an eight-year-old girl. He was suspended for a game and fined. Barkley took responsibility for his actions and deeply reflected on his behavior. In an interview, Barkley admitted that he was blaming other people and circumstances for his actions instead of looking in the mirror. He also acknowledged that he was so focused on winning at any cost that he wasn't respecting the game or his own talent. He apologized to the girl and her family and developed a friendship with them. Barkley realized that he didn't have to respond to hecklers or blame anyone for his own feelings or behavior. By taking responsibility, he bounced back from that incident and was a better person and basketball player.

I am not a big fan of advice that states, "Hey, just flip that switch and be perfect and stay perfect" as a way to overcome difficulties and be an ultra-productive and highly motivated person. It just does not work that way for me. As much as I would like to claim that I am

100% resistant to internal, social, and environmental factors that can get me off track at times, I must accept that I am not. Sometimes, it is easy to get right back on track and other times it is quite difficult. It can be a process of analyzing those factors that are affecting me through reflection and introspection and it does take some time. Ultimately, we all want to develop a high level of resilience and not be impacted at all or, at the very least, for a noticeably short time regarding situations, circumstances, and even people that can bring us down. Be grateful for the opportunities presented that allow you to learn and to improve yourself and do not get down on yourself even more if it takes some time. By taking responsibility for your progress, you will keep working through those rough times to get better, and soon you will be bouncing back so fast that you will not even remember how you used to be bothered by them.

Change is the single most reliable and predictable factor in my life. I cannot be anything but grateful for it.

CHAPTER 3: IMPROVEMENT

I am constantly striving to improve in three areas: relationships, knowledge, and skills. By creating, maintaining, and strengthening relationships, I feel better about myself and the world around me. Relationships are more than just tools of influence that help us to get what we want. They are connections that define who we are in this world: appreciate and nurture your relationships. Please understand, I do not mean you have to have a relationship to define yourself. What I am implying here is to look at your current relationships to understand them on a deeper level. Who do you attract into your life? What is the relationship like? Is it shallow or deep? Harmonious or full of conflict? We can glean a lot about ourselves by looking at our relationships. Additionally, I believe we should seek knowledge and find ways to apply what we learn. While this seems obvious, it is easier said than done. We should realize the importance of appreciating the successes at hand while always striving to learn more and trying to improve. We should seek balance while continually pushing the boundaries to a measured amount that keeps us within a believable goal. It is about knowing the risk and understanding our fears, while taking the action necessary that will lead us to a better state. It's a desire to improve ourselves and to help others become better in some way.

I am a huge proponent of developing a high level of self-awareness. However, it can be a long, difficult, and painful journey. Depending on where we currently stand on the path of self-awareness, it may be difficult to know where and how to get started. One way is to simply look around. We can take a good look at our relationships, our current situation, and the surrounding circumstances. Simply put, what we will see is a reflection of what we are projecting. Now, it will take more than just a good look. We are going to have to put some thought into it. We are going to have to try to look at what is going on in our lives as objectively as we possibly can. This can be very difficult because most of us tend to have biases. These biases can be based on our beliefs and conditioning which serve as filters that affect how we interpret the world. One possible way to become *more* objective is to think about how we feel about our relationships, financial situation, occupation, etc. If something feels good or right, then chances are we are projecting good vibes (e.g., what we say and how we say it).

Additionally, our behavior and decisions tend to corroborate and support those good feelings. Conversely, if something feels bad or wrong, then we may be projecting bad vibes. We should pay close attention to how people respond to us and the outcomes of our decisions. Hey, I understand that sometimes people may negatively respond to us and it's all about what they're projecting (do we respond in turn or take a different approach?). I also know that feelings can be tricky because we can manipulate ourselves: We are good at rationalizing and justifying. And sometimes we have to take a stand – I get that. But, if we will listen closely to those who care about us and take a hard look at the circumstances in our lives, we can learn a lot about ourselves.

By the way, do you know what "triggers" you? A trigger is a stimulus that can affect any of the senses and causes a conditioned response based upon a previous event that is associated with some degree of trauma. It is a very personal matter and can vary in degree based on the experienced trauma, the extent of possible abuse, how it impacted you, and how you coped with it. For me, it is usually based on what someone says, their behavior, or a combination of the two.

As an example, if a parent or an adult taunted you as a child, you may have gotten angry and when you expressed that anger, you were "put in your place." And when that parent verbally berates you for something you did, you were conditioned to know that if you did not change your behavior quickly that the taunting would be escalated. The next time you were taunted, you probably may have been afraid to express your anger and so your emotional outlet was to cry. If the adult got upset or made fun of you for crying, then the next time you were provoked, you didn't feel like you could express how this made you feel based on the previous interactions and as a child you don't have the level of emotional control and verbal acuity to talk through it, so you chose to suppress your feelings, bottle them up, show no emotion, and not act out in any way. And you will behave this way toward the adult for quite some time, maybe hours or days and at some point, they are nice to you again. So now you associate this behavior with how the adult wants you to behave, and you are rewarded. However, on the inside you were angry and hurt. You internalized the event and carried on a dialogue in your head trying to understand why someone would do this and why you feel the way you do. You cry in secret. Furthermore, you might express your anger at inanimate objects. You may have no one else to talk to, so you try to work it out in your head. This happens repeatedly.

The problem is that you have an extremely limited perspective on the emotional, cognitive, and behavioral impression these events have on you and how to properly work through them. At some point to answer these questions, you convince yourself that you deserved it. You do not know exactly why, but there must have been something you did to deserve this treatment from this authority figure. After convincing yourself that you deserve it, you now feel inferior in some way. This feeling of inferiority affects your behavior. You start acting as though you are inferior. But you are self-aware enough to know something is off, and you do not like this feeling.

So now you work on building your confidence and self-esteem, but you are not sure how to do it. You compliment and praise yourself for the smallest of acts. You long for this from someone else and desire that external validation. At some point, you just want to be liked by everyone, so they won't be mean to you. You learn to laugh a lot, be funny, and please people. Guess what? Because a trigger can be something that reminds you of the original event, every time you are taunted, criticized, mocked, or teased by someone, you are triggered. This trigger can have an impact through your adulthood. You follow this emotional, cognitive, and behavioral pattern of bottling up and shutting down, while carrying the same internal dialogue. You wonder if you deserved it, and as a response, you try to be likable by pleasing the other person, giving yourself praise for what you can, and waiting to be rewarded for good behavior. As you can see from this example, layers upon layers have been created to hide that something has upset you, or you've had your feelings hurt. And you have done it so many times that it is automatic and over time, you justify your behavior and will defend it.

Let me outline a specific example that may or may not apply, or maybe parts of it do. What if you are in a relationship, and you have a partner who says something to you that triggers you? Maybe they are truly criticizing, insulting, or mocking you in some way, or you may simply be perceiving them as doing so. If you haven't worked on this part of yourself to understand your reaction or why you are behaving a certain way, then you will follow the same pattern, until you decide to change. What if your partner doesn't understand why you've reacted this way? They may be oblivious to what they said and how they said something and that it was a trigger for you. And what if part or all of your reaction is a trigger for them and they have a reactive process that they are going through?

They may explicitly state they are upset with your behavior, and then when you explain that you didn't like what they said or how they said something to you, they tell you it's your problem. You are too sensitive, or there is something wrong with you. Now you loop back through feeling inferior, trying to please the other person, giving yourself praise, and waiting to be rewarded. But, it doesn't come.

Instead, your partner is not budging. Because you are stuck in this process, you now don't feel that you can open up to your partner about how they have affected you, and you shut down even more. In your mind, they are the problem, and you don't want to talk about it. Whether you try to explain or shut down, they continue to tell you that something is wrong with you. They may even think you are doing something purposeful or have some kind of disorder, and it is based in their own reactive pattern to being triggered by you. Now the two of you are stuck in a loop. This is obviously a bad situation. Again, this is one specific example. Sometimes, there is a lot of compassion, understanding, and communication which is key to working through these types of issues.

At this point, I believe it is important to take your responsibility for your own behavior and focus on that. Forget about blaming the other person. By taking responsibility for yourself, you open the door for taking control of disrupting this process. You need to start peeling back the layers and understanding what you are doing, why it is happening, and make your way to the source. It may happen quickly, within a few days or weeks, or it may take a long time, even months or years. Either way, don't be hard on yourself. Remember, it depends on several factors.

There is an abundance of books, videos, and podcasts that can help you. There are many resources at your fingertips to begin your path of healing. Therapy may help, but if you set the intention and become keenly aware of your behavior, trace it back to the trigger, and eventually to the source, then you can heal yourself. Then and only then can you really see what may have been triggers that caused your partner and even your parent to behave in the ways that they did and possibly explore their own past to better understand. They may not have had the awareness and opportunity to heal like you have. We are all capable of doing this. What's stopping us? Are we in our own way? We should not be afraid to look in the mirror and acknowledge our angry or hurt inner child. Now is the time to be there for yourself. Be the person your inner child never had.

If we want to dive in a little deeper, we can do what is called "shadow work." The shadow part of ourselves refers to that which we hide from the world, deny, repress, and often lies totally unexamined. I do not claim to have done this extensively, but I have worked on it to some degree. I had to take a hard look at some of my insecurities and not- so- admirable behaviors, accept them as part of my personality, and think about what is at the core of each. These characteristics were hard to admit, and it was uncomfortable to reveal what lay beneath. Here are four that I examined, along with applying GRIP concepts:

- I want to be recognized for my intellectual abilities because I am worried people will think I am not qualified to discuss, write, or do the things I really want to do. Therefore, I keep creating my own credibility hurdles to keep myself down and I never feel good enough. I had to think through this more. I asked myself why someone's opinion matters so much. Why is it important that someone acknowledges my intellectual abilities? Do I want to feel special? Do I like the attention? What does it really mean if someone thinks I'm not qualified? Is it rooted in my childhood when I was told I couldn't or wouldn't be able to accomplish a goal? Do I feel criticized? Regardless, I take responsibility for the feelings I have concerning this so-called need, and this empowers me. Now, I can recognize those feelings and realize that they do not have any real power over me. It is just in my imagination. It is okay to accept constructive criticism that is meant to help me, and it is also okay to distance myself from negativity. When I allow myself to just be with all the facets that make me who I am, then I can shine my best and for this, I am grateful.

- I want someone to understand me because I do not think anyone really can, but I make it difficult for people because I do not open myself up. I am worried that the real me is unlikable, but that means there are parts of me that I do not always like, even though I try to accept myself wholly and unconditionally. For every perceived flaw, there is potential for growth. What if there are people who understand me, but I shut them out because of my own fears? I can accept myself for all my positive characteristics, strengths, dark sides, and opportunities for growth. This is the balance I seek. Introspection while not being self-absorbed and taking action with the right amount of planning and reflection to learn from my experiences.

- I am compassionate with myself and other people, but I sometimes do not push myself or others to be better because I can be afraid of failing and I project that onto other people. Therefore, I give others an out. I will tend to define this as an aspect of loving someone and how I want to be loved in return, but it comes across as me not caring. It is really because I want to avoid the negative feelings of stress and anxiety from being pushed too hard, so I can be avoidant at times and not set tough goals for myself. Realizing this opens the door for interrupting these tendencies, pushing myself, and continuing to be compassionate as needed. Incremental growth is still growth.

- I want to be recognized as attractive so I create situations where I can receive positive feedback from others, such as on social media. This is because I am sometimes insecure with how I look and seek external validation. I hide from this by saying beauty is on the inside, but I think there are times when I can be ugly on the inside and so I use my outer appearance to try and cover up that about myself which I do not want others to see. Then I must ask myself why it matters. What do I get from this that really nourishes my heart, mind, and soul? Whatever it may be, it is fleeting. Being physically attractive is meaningless if my heart isn't in the right place. I should care less about how I look while at the same time continue taking good care of myself. I should continuously work on building my character and acting in a way that is in alignment with my values and what I care about most.

I am being vulnerable in sharing these, but I hope you see how bringing these to light can help us to not only manage them but redirect them in more positive ways. Being able to admit these factors is very empowering. So, what do we do with this information? By taking responsibility, setting our intention on improving, seeking out the resources we need, and creating self-development goals, we begin moving in the right direction. In the end, being authentic and true to ourselves, allowing our positivity to flow, opening up to the wonderful people in our lives, and harboring no fear of loving, no matter what. That is the fountain from which true success, recognition, and high vibration comes. We can have someone in our life who sees us for who we are, loves and supports us, helps us to evolve, grow and get better, and we can do the same for them. Let's not allow our pasts to weigh us down. Let's learn from it and move forward better than we were.

Goal Setting

Personally, I am not happy unless I am pursuing a goal. That does not mean I become so completely obsessed with it such that I allow other aspects of my life to become out of balance, but I just feel like I am at least chipping away at it. The problem for me is that I will ask myself questions like, "Is this the right goal for me?" or, "Does this goal contribute to my overall purpose?" Honestly, sometimes I am not sure about the answers. However, if (a) the goal is sufficiently challenging and believable, (b) I feel like I'm improving in some way, (c) working on the goal will add or complement a skill or characteristic that can be useful in the future, and (d) it is aligned with at least one tenet regarding my philosophy on life, then I feel good about pursuing the goal. Of course, it can be all too easy to fill in the blanks as needed if there is a strong bias for the goal and it is always important to check the necessary actions against one's ethical framework. Regardless, I feel it is important to ask these questions and answer them as honestly as possible. Internal issues will affect one's motivation over time more than anything else, so inner work is necessary.

Decades of research on goal setting strongly suggests a positive relationship between the skillful setting of goals and performance. To answer why goal setting is such an effective tool, let us look at some professionally researched points. First, a goal, whether prescribed by someone else or self-prescribed, sets a level of performance and/or an outcome that we want to achieve. And we must truly want it or the goal will not stick. Second, a goal gives us a clear picture of where we are now versus where we want to be. There is a discrepancy that we want to fix and there is discontent with our present state. This is the main driver of our efforts! This brings to light how a stated goal illuminates the gap between a current state and a desired future state and how an awareness of that gap can motivate performance levels and strategies to achieve the desired future state.

What do we need when we set out on our goal? First, we need commitment to the goal, which can be enhanced by our self-efficacy.

Remember that? We need to believe in our ability to perform the necessary tasks. The better we believe it, the better the commitment. This leads to the next point. We need to understand the tasks necessary to attain our goal. Third, we need to be aware of any constraints on resources that will possibly affect performance. Last, we need feedback on how to track our progress objectively. Be careful of those biases! When we are confronted with a goal, we tap into our knowledge and skills; we use deliberate planning, and develop task strategies using both cognitive and behavioral mechanisms, that serve to direct attention and effort towards behaviors that support our goal.

There is strong evidence from an abundance of research that setting goals can have a positive impact on our lives; however, when goal setting is not conducted properly, undesirable outcomes can occur. I have outlined ten potential pitfalls from the research in goal setting and ways to overcome them. These potential pitfalls, if not corrected, can be the reason for missed objectives and a significant failure: (a) not enough knowledge, (b) conflicting goals, (c) negatively framed goals, (d) punishment for failing to achieve a goal, (e) relying on previous success strategies, (f) money as a motivator, (g) goal is tied to self-esteem, (h) ignoring other performance areas, (i) stretched too far, and (j) ever-increasing difficult goals.

The first potential problem is when we lack the knowledge needed to achieve a performance goal. In this case, it is best to give specific learning goals that support the performance goal. The second is when we have conflicting goals. Our behavior is split and not directed toward one. The third is when the goal is framed in a negative perspective and viewed as some kind of threat. Fourth is when punishment is used when the goal is not attained. Errors and failures will always occur when setting and pursuing difficult and challenging goals. Fear of failure can discourage us from setting and achieving a goal. The fifth is when we rely too heavily on past strategies from previous successes and then misapplying them to even more challenging goals. One way to counteract the misapplication of past strategies to a current situation is to set sub-goals that support the longer-term goal. The sixth potential problem lies with money as a motivator to attain a goal. We are more likely to overstate our performance when we are just shy of attaining our goal. We may focus too heavily on making the numbers look good instead of the results. We can also find ways to make an easy goal appear to be difficult when motivated by monetary gain. A seventh issue is when a goal is tied to self-esteem which can lead to irrational and risky behavior. Thus, the goal may not be abandoned even in the face of overwhelming evidence that it should be. An eighth potential problem is when performance that isn't perceived as part of the goal is ignored. It must be clear as to what outcomes are necessary for the goal attainment. A ninth possible concern is when we have stretched too far with the number of goals set and we experience increased stress. The final potential pitfall is when unattainable goals are set when we have attained a challenging goal in the past. When progressively harder and harder goals are set, it can be perceived as punishment. As high-performing individuals, we should set our goals appropriately so that they will lead to success.

Risks associated with improper goal setting include (a) having too many goals, (b) inappropriate timelines, (c) goals that are too challenging, (d) promotion of unethical behavior, (e) psychological effects of goal failure, (g) not having learning goals, (h) creating a competitive environment, (i) diminishing intrinsic motivation, (j) not individualizing goals, and (k) having too narrow of a focus. We need to learn how to set and when to set goals through training and risk mitigation. Goal setting is a well-researched and useful tool for attaining desired outcomes but can have there is the potential for detrimental consequences for us when misunderstood. Coaching is a method to help us with goal-setting strategies to improve performance.

Goal setting is close to my heart. I wrote my master's thesis on the topic of goal setting in 2012 and selected it because of the profound effects I had experienced. I truly believed that I could help others who were struggling to achieve their goals. I started my research in late 2010 by reading numerous articles and books about goal setting. I would listen to audiobooks nearly nonstop on the subject. I took away some valuable points, but I had my own ideas, as well.

For my research, I conducted an experiment wherein I chose three different developmental algebra sections that were taught by the same instructor, but at different times. I felt that if developmental algebra students could benefit from goal setting, then anyone could. Many of these students struggled with low self-esteem, math anxiety, and just did not believe they could ever pass an algebra class. One of the classes served as the control group and the other two were the treatment groups. Of these two groups, members in one class had the goal of an A-grade prescribed for their next test and the other group chose their own goal. I hypothesized that students with either a prescribed or self-created goal on a test would score significantly better than students without a goal. Based on the results of this experiment, I was wrong. However, something more interesting happened.

Before I experimented, I had recorded their previous test scores. I was also curious about how the students would perform after the goals were set relative to before. The treatment was me giving a goal-setting class that I had developed. It had a logical flow and was motivational in tone (I'm aware that this was a fundamental weakness in my research, and aptly named the experimenter effect). First, here's what I asked the students:

1. How many of you have a goal to earn an A on the next test? (Only a few raised their hands.)
2. For those of you who have the goal, how many of you believe you *can* earn an A on the next test? (Even fewer)
3. For those of you who believe you can, how many of you believe that you *will* earn an A on the next test? (Just a couple of students)
4. For those of you who believe you will, *why* do you believe it?

As they told me their reasons, I listed them on the board. Many of them were simple tasks that made good sense such as attending class, studying, and keeping up with assignments and some were behaviors such as asking for help when needed.

Next, I asked, "What are some things that could keep you from accomplishing the above tasks?" This list was negations of the previous items, e.g., **not** attending class, **not** keeping up with assignments, etc. Then, I asked, "What motivates you to overcome roadblocks and resist choices that could compromise the achievement of your goal?"

Here's where it got interesting. This is where the students started showing some passion. They were sharing their purpose. There were statements like "because I have high expectations of myself" or "because I want to make my family proud" or "because I want a good job when I graduate." Now, these may not have the ring of profoundness that some may expect, but that does not matter. It was *their* purpose, and it was something they could tap into when things got tough and that would motivate them. Some were intrinsic and somewhere extrinsic. Regardless, each had a purpose that could be verbalized with intensity.

Now, I wanted to hear from those who did not believe they could make an A on the next test. So, I asked them, "Of those that did not believe they could make an A, why do you not believe you can do it?"

Their list of items matched the list that was created by the "believers" when they were asked what would keep them from accomplishing the tasks that would help them to achieve an A. They didn't even realize it! When I pointed it out, they saw the relationship. Then, when I pointed to what the "A" believers were going to do to overcome roadblocks and resist choices that would impede their goal, they got it.

If there was a "what" that they wanted to accomplish, then they needed a "how" to get them there. And when they felt shaky, they needed to revisit their "why" and it needed to be strong. The below triangle is a visual representation. The "what" they want to accomplish must be clear and they must desire it. Then, they will figure out the "how" or they will seek the help they need. The "why" is their foundation and must be solid.

WHAT
HOW
WHY

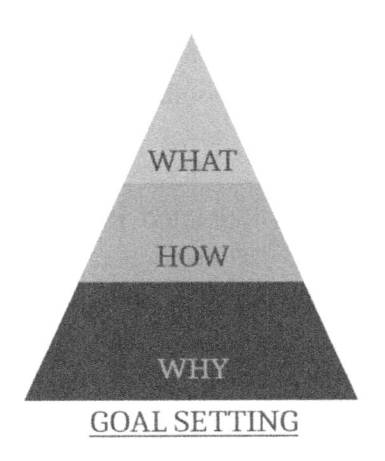

<u>GOAL SETTING</u>

But it is not that easy. It comes back to beliefs. If they did not truly believe they could achieve the A, then their behaviors would support the limiting belief and they would follow the list that they created that they said would keep them from it. They had to see that they were in control. If they changed their behaviors to match what the students were going to do to achieve an A, then they also could achieve an A. If you want to be successful, do what successful people do!

I explained to them that some will set a goal, but they will not believe it. Deep inside, they have doubts. They will self-sabotage and not be fully aware they are doing so. They will make choices that do not support their stated goals but instead support their *true beliefs*. This causes dissonance and they must find a way to resolve it. Without this awareness, they tend to blame other people (the instructor), events (friends came over), and circumstances (time of day, schedule, etc.) for their behaviors and negative outcomes. By not taking responsibility, they do not feel in control and will not focus on what they can do to overcome potential obstacles. They will not bring to mind their *purpose* to help motivate them. It is a self-fulfilling prophecy based on self-limiting beliefs that they ultimately resist coming to terms with because that would be counter to their beliefs!

Does this remind you of something? Think about what we discussed before: ability – performance – fixed mindset vs. effort– mastery – growth mindset. If we do not believe in ourselves or have a fear of something that is holding us back and we are convinced that we must have the ability to do something to be successful and our motivation, such as an A grade, is hinging on our performance (and we just so happen to set ourselves up for a poor grade), then we need to see this is a fixed mindset. And could this be a reason we do not believe in ourselves in the first place? However, even in the face of fears, if we get started to put forth great effort to master the topic regardless of a grade (which, ironically, will most likely be a good grade), then we have a growth mindset! We will see setbacks and failures for just simply feedback on our effort and level of mastery which we know takes time and we will increase our effort and adaptive behaviors such as seeking help and we will grow!

We tend to defend our habits. With repetition, the neural pathways that are created to perform certain routines are strengthened so that we can go on "autopilot" and free up our cognitive resources for other things that come into our awareness. If we have a habit of self-defeat, then we do it without even thinking about it. We tend to resist change even if it is for the better. We must overcome it! To help overcome it, we must realize that these self-limiting beliefs are all that is holding us back. We must believe that we can change. We must not let temporary defeats and failures control our thoughts, which results in us telling ourselves, and then tell ourselves "See, I told you that you couldn't do it!" and then we slip back into the old ways of thinking that support our self-limiting beliefs.

Most of the students understood and accepted this logic, but there were still some who thought that no matter what they did, they were not going to achieve the A. I asked them, "Why?"

The responses boiled down to two things: fear of failure and fear of criticism. These fears were fueling the fire of their self-limiting beliefs. How these fears and self-limiting beliefs were formed did not matter as much as trying to help them overcome it. I told them that when something is suggested by someone else or self-suggested over and over, it can become a belief. Then, thoughts are formed that support the belief. What is said when talking to others endorses the belief. External evidence is sought out to support it. The world is viewed through the lens of belief. Confirmation bias is extremely powerful.

I explained that they must take control of their thoughts and improve their self-talk. They should use the power of repetition to their benefit and tell themselves "I am in control of my thoughts" or "I can do it" or "I will do what it takes within the boundaries of my values to be successful." This may feel strange to them at first, but it is because their current thoughts, that support the self-limiting beliefs, are deeply ingrained.

It is important to remember that temporary defeat and failure are based on a perception of an outcome of an event that does not define who we are. Understand the causes and make a plan to overcome them. This is a learning process and takes time. It takes patience. We must be patient with ourselves. It is vital to our success.

So, whether I prescribed a goal of an A-grade on their next test or they created the goal themselves, I told them to write it down. I had created a goal statement sheet that was ready for them to use. It stated the goal or the "what," the actions they were going to take, or the "how," and their purpose, or "why." I also included some positive affirmations and instructions to read the statements, visualize the goal being achieved, and virtually experience the feeling of success. I told them to visualize being handed back their test and seeing the A. And to allow themselves to feel that good feeling when seeing it. I even gave them a checklist to help them remember to do as they did this every morning and night.

What do you think happened? The two classes with goals didn't outperform the class without a goal on their test that was taken after the goal-setting class (for whatever reason, the randomly assigned control group had a higher pretest average), but the classes with a goal significantly outperformed their previous test scores. Not only were the scores significantly higher, but the test score variation among the students reduced significantly. A graph of their scores is below. Group 1 was the control group, Group 2 was prescribed a goal, and Group 3 chose their own goal.

Interval Plot of Pre, Post
95% CI for the Mean

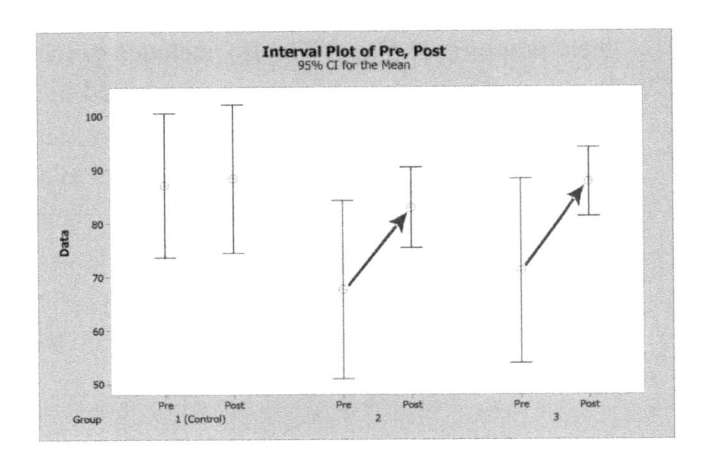

For me, this is incredible. To see nearly the same results from two separate classes is hugely significant. When I have followed a good process, goal setting has worked for me. Granted, I have had my ups and downs with goal setting. I had read about all the positives and negatives and sometimes I was not sure if it was all hype. But the results of this research strongly suggest that goal setting can help students who are in a developmental algebra class and to me, that is amazing. I must admit, I have set a personal goal of helping more people benefit from the power of goal setting.

Emotional Intelligence

We can also experience failures when our behavior is rooted in emotional and behavioral issues. If we have poor Emotional Intelligence (EI), relationships may suffer. EI encompasses the following five skills: (a) self-awareness, (b) self-regulation, (c) motivation, (d) empathy, and (e) social awareness. To simplify, we have personal competence consisting of self-awareness and self-management skills, and social competence that includes social awareness and relationship management skills.

If we have a high degree of self-awareness, then we can accurately detect emotions, understand how those emotions manifest, and also understand how these emotions affect us and others. Being self-aware includes knowing our strengths, weaknesses, motivations, goals, and values. If we lack self-awareness, then we are generally unaware of our strengths and weaknesses and may accept challenges that require impressive skills in areas where we are weak, ultimately failing to meet our goals. Low self-awareness leads to inaccurate self-assessments, being resistant or be unaccepting of feedback, having low self-confidence, and not asking for help when it is needed at critical times. Self-awareness is so important for overall performance that most people rich in self-awareness are top performers.

Self-management is a natural extension of self-awareness and entails conscientious choices about actions and behavior. Being unaware of our weaknesses, emotions, moods, motivations, and impulses makes it practically impossible to manage them. Self-regulation frees us from feeling like we have no control over how emotions affect us. It is about controlling our impulses, emotional reactions, judgments, verbal responses, and exercising restraint when the situation calls for it. If we lack self-management in these areas, then an environment of distrust and unfairness is created. it creates an environment of distrust and unfairness. Outbursts of anger and heavy mood swings affect our ability to think clearly and influence our behaviors. Low impulse control often leads to poor decisions. Impulsive behavior is a direct indicator of poor emotional regulation and lack of self-management.

The inability to handle change and uncertainty in our environment is another effect of a deficiency in self-management. The rapid change in the absence of self-control can cause a negative emotional reaction resulting in panic, poor communication, and a lack of rational thinking. Rigidity, which is the inability or unwillingness to adapt to change, is an indication that we will probably experience a failure to achieve our goals. Without sufficient self-management, there is an inability to use awareness of emotions to stay flexible and direct behavior positively. The absence of personal competence in the areas of self-awareness and self-management materializes as the inability to lead ourselves properly, the generation of poor decisions, and the creation of a negative environment.

Social competence includes social awareness and relationship management. Social awareness refers to us recognizing others' emotions and behaviors while attempting to understand their situation; it is an outward focus using observation skills instead of focusing inward. It is about having empathy toward others and considering others' feelings as part of making intelligent decisions. However, we should not fear making tough decisions and providing negative feedback when needed. Performance feedback, even when negative, is important for us to be fully aware of goal progression and whether or not we need to make changes. We can have high expectations of ourselves and hold ourselves accountable when necessary while continuing to exercise empathy for those around us.

Relationship management is the culmination of the other EI skills. When we understand and manage our own emotions, we have an awareness of our strengths and weaknesses, we better control our impulses, exercise empathy, and listen well to others more attentively. We will tend to have better working relationships with others. However, the inverse is also true: A deficiency in the areas of self-awareness, self-management, and social skills can result in poor working relationships with others.

An essential communication skill that should be practiced and continuously improved upon is listening. When we lack good listening skills, it is a characteristic of poor social awareness. When we are preoccupied with our thoughts, electronic devices, or anything other than the people who we should be focused on and listening to during a conversation, we subconsciously communicate that others are not important enough to warrant our attention. This negatively affects our relationships that we have with others and can lead to resentment, poor teamwork, poor performance, and failing at attaining our goals.

I am convinced that there are some important characteristics and attributes that people must incorporate into their mindset to help them achieve a long-term goal. These are vision, belief, consistency, and resilience. It is important to visualize what you want to achieve. At least create a rough draft in your mind. This will get you excited and anxious to get started. However, nothing will deter you from getting started more than a lack of belief in yourself and your abilities to achieve it. Therefore, you must develop a strategy that includes sub-goals that are believable, and these will lay out the path to your true goal.

Now, I do not necessarily believe that if you just visualize and believe in your goal that it will simply fall into your lap, but I do believe that doing so will open doors for you, allowing you to take action and pay attention to opportunities that will help you. Some people will be excited at first and then when that excitement wears off or they are not seeing results fast enough, they will stop working toward the goal. So, consistency is key. Keep going even if it is a small step each day. Finally, there will be obstacles, deterrents, and setbacks. You might feel down at times and feel like stopping, but do not let these things keep you down. Bounce back and keep moving. Keep inching toward the finish line and before you know it, your goal will be easier to see, your beliefs will strengthen, you will work harder, and nothing will stop you.

To be an inspiration to someone else
is an inspiration in itself.
Be thankful when people see
something in you that makes them believe.

CHAPTER 4: POSITIVITY

I used to think that I needed to be positive all the time and it was to the point that I would not even allow myself to feel anything "negative." But that was just a lie because I was suppressing those feelings that I had labeled as negative. At some point, they would make their way out. So, I had to learn two things: (a) stop labeling the feelings as positive and negative in the traditional sense of good versus bad and (b) realize there is a big difference between what I feel and how I behave. However, naming and accepting a feeling immediately brings a sense of power over how it is interpreted and any reaction to it. I like to think that feelings are embedded with important information but must be looked at with as much objectivity as possible. This can be difficult because I can be engulfed by the feeling and, therefore, biased. Also, there is a big difference between a feeling that may have been labeled as negative and behaving negatively. For me, the behavior is what matters and ultimately, I am in control of it. When I don't behave the way I think I should have, then I shouldn't blame the feeling and instead, I should take responsibility and commit to doing better the next time. This a process of moving in a positive direction, which is what I wanted to begin with from the start.

Do you ever feel a sense of discontentment? Do you ever get a feeling deep down in the center of your chest that seems presents itself as a longing of sorts? It is like a feeling that there's something important to be done, but you don't know for sure what and so the feeling is one of anticipation for something exciting, mixed with anxiety because you can't figure it out. Maybe that's why we keep trying new things with the hope that our path is revealed through the actions that we take. For us, failure was just a way of learning what path not to take. And we have faith that both the means and the end are in alignment with something bigger than ourselves. For me, the feeling comes and goes, waxes and wanes, but never goes away completely. It is like destiny keeps whispering in my ear, but I cannot quite make out the words. It is like a thirst that demands to be quenched. When it comes right down to it, I am just a guy who keeps trying.

When that feeling creeps in on me, I always ask the question, "Am I just bored or is there something more for which I should be striving?" The answer is not always clear and if I'm not careful, the feeling of discontentment and confusion may lead to a depressed mood and then a short-lived state of apathy. There is a natural inclination for me to be positive and optimistic, so I will always get out of it, but I do not like going there in the first place.

But I sometimes find it difficult to balance being grateful for what I have against a level of discontent that constantly reminds me to strive for something more. I must remind myself how grateful I should be for all the wonderful things in my life while continuously doing something, no matter how small, to get me a little closer to my goal. I can beam impatient at times because I feel like I should already be there while simultaneously finding myself inside my head to the point where I am not taking enough action. However, solace can be found when remembering that creating a sculpture from stone requires chipping away the parts that do not belong, and, over time, one's vision will be revealed. I think the key for me is to acknowledge the discontentment as a part of me that keeps pushing for something better and at the same time remain grateful for all the wonderful things in my life and opportunities in my life to work towards and, if nothing else, a better version of me. And that turns it around almost immediately. I say, "Let it flow and let it go."

I do not know about you, but I have high expectations when it comes to my behavior. Now, I understand not everyone has the same values, morals, beliefs, etc. which tend to govern each individual's thoughts on how to behave in a variety of situations and scenarios, but I'm talking more about how I treat people. You know, I am talking about anything from basic interaction to deep conversations. But, no matter how hard I try, sometimes I fall short. I do not fall flat on my face like I may have done on occasion in the distant past, but I can still be self-critical if I allow myself to vary too much from my expectations.

As an example, do you ever get frustrated? I do on occasion and even though I am much better at controlling it, there are times when there will be a verbal slip of how I am feeling. A big difference these days is that I do not beat myself up over it like I used to do. I simply take responsibility for my actions, apologize when I have the opportunity, forgive myself for my shortcomings, and think about how to better handle it next time. Perfection is subjective and is an ideal state that we accept as unattainable, but we can always get better a little at a time.

As you can tell, a recurring theme for me is balance. There is a quote from Osho which states to accept ourselves as we are and to realize that we are good regardless of what others may have led us to believe. There is also a quote by Rumi which implies that when we are doing soul work, some truths may be "searing" and are meant to help us as opposed to just words of simple solace or comforting in nature. So, where is the balance?

For me, it is about being okay with myself *and* who I want to be, flaws and all.

It is about finding reasons to be grateful, happy, and positive without ignoring or avoiding traits and characteristics that cause myself and other people problems that I want to either eradicate or improve upon. For example, as part of a holistic approach to self-improvement, I engage in fitness activities, enjoying nature, reading, writing, etc., and I have also had sessions with a therapist to work on improving those "dark" areas of my personality. Why? Because a searing truth may burn momentarily, but not as bad as the fires started that can burn others by ignoring those truths.

However, I beg you to remember, "energy flows where attention goes" so focus on the person you want to be, never stop incrementally improving in some way, don't ignore the dark parts of yourself just to avoid feeling bad, be grateful for all the good you have to offer, and accept yourself for the wonderful person you are and can become. But is there something more we can do?

Self-Regulation

Aristotle suggested that positive human character is portrayed when emotions are expressed in the correct way, to the correct extent, on the correct occasions, and about the right things. This suggests that the appropriateness of both positive and negative emotions are dependent, to some degree, on contextual factors (e.g., laughter is appropriate after hearing a joke, but not at a funeral, and anger is appropriate when an injustice has occurred, but not after receiving a sincere compliment). However, when we suffer a failure or setback, then we can experience heightened and prolonged negative emotions such as depression or grief. How we manage these negative emotions can affect our ability to learn, adapt, and bounce back.

In general, there are three underlying cognitive components to self-regulation: (a) self-observation, (b) a judgmental process, and (c) self-response. However, if we cannot exercise control over our motivation and behavior, then intention and desire have little effect. It's not if we fail, but when we fail, and if we are unable to regulate our emotions, then we may become severely depressed. After failure, we may experience bouts of embarrassment and grief, and quickly move on, but other times we may allow failure to affect our self-esteem and confidence. The goal is to move toward recovery instead of a state of paralysis or downward spiral.

After experiencing a failure or setback, resilience can be a time of transition whereof reflection, analysis, reappraisals, new goals are formed, and action occurs within the cognitive, emotional, and behavioral domains that tend to have an optimistic slant. Recovery from failure can be seen as a process composed of three phases. First, there is an initial period wherein which we remove ourselves psychologically from the failure to heal. Second, we need time to reflect and make sense of the failure. Finally, we must take action to move on from the failure. Therefore, through exercising self-regulation, we can summon our motivation and activate the necessary cognitive resources to plan a course of action so that we might overcome failure.

Emotion Regulation

Emotions arise when we pay attention to a situation and appraise it as being immediately relevant to our currently active circumstances or goals. Typically, emotions are brought forth when we evaluate a situation as having important challenges or opportunities and will affect our experience, behavior, and physiology to some degree. Emotions have three main features: (a) meaning that we have introduced through appraisal of a situation, (b) contain experiential, behavioral, and physiological elements, and (c) have both important and sensitive qualities.

Emotion regulation is the processes by which we influence which emotions we have when we have them, and how we experience and express them. Emotion regulation begins with either an explicit or implicit goal to influence the generation of emotions and often involves reducing negative emotions (e.g., anger, sadness, etc.) or increasing positive emotions (e.g., love, joy, etc.).

Taken from a well-researched process model of emotion regulation, five emotion regulation strategies occur along the emotion generation continuum that we can use in our favor:

1. Situation Selection (SS): Requires some degree of self-awareness and being able to see the features of given situations along with how we tend to respond. Then, we can actively engage ourselves in situations where predicted emotional responses are desired and avoid situations where emotions are unwanted.

2. Situation Modification (SM): Here is where we modify or change the external environment of a situation (e.g., changing the lighting and music for a romantic interest or leaving an area if someone enters that is disliked). There can be some overlap with situation selection because modifying a situation may effectively create a new situation that is either desired or unwanted.

3. Attentional Deployment (AD): This is where we change our internal focus in a given situation to redirect attention by

using strategies such as distraction where attention is shifted, e.g. thoughts are invoked that are unrelated to a situation or gazing upon a different scene that lessens an emotional impact; or rumination where a focus on thoughts and feelings are sustained to the point of increasing the duration and intensity of emotion which can be positive or negative.

4. Cognitive Change (CC): Refers to changing an appraisal or evaluation of a situation such that the thoughts and meaning of the situation are different which in turn elicits a different emotional response. Reappraisal is a common form of cognitively oriented emotional regulation and tends to lead to decreased levels of negative emotions, increased levels of positive emotions, and has virtually no impact on memory and no social disruption.

5. Response Modulation (RM): Refers to directly influencing the physiological, behavioral, or experiential aspects of emotion with such tactics as exercise and drugs. There are positive and negative

ways to do this. A positive way might be through meditating. A negative way might be through suppression SS, SM, AD, and CC are referred to as antecedent focused because these would occur before the emotion is generated and RM is response focused because it is performed after the emotion has been felt. Any of these tactics can change the external or internal environment such that we may loop back to the beginning where we have the choice to stay or leave. SS and SM involve changing or altering the environment in which an emotional response is likely to occur, while AD, CC, and RM are cognitive and behavioral strategies to regulate emotions that have been experienced to some degree. What does this mean? It means we probably have a lot more control than we give ourselves credit. We have the power to change ourselves into a more positive state of mind.

A lot of common major stressful events, such as the unexpected loss of a job, are generally associated with a wide range of negative outcomes. Emotion regulation can moderate the relationship between stress and resilience. Another researched model boils it down to two aspects: attention control (AC) and cognitive reappraisal (CR). AC consists of focusing attention toward or away from either internal or external stimuli. Depending on how AC is strategically used, it may lead to negative or positive outcomes. Distraction or rumination can lead to negative outcomes while a different response where irrelevant negative information is safely ignored, and relevant or changeable information is attended to and coped with appropriately such as using active problem-solving leads to more positive outcomes. CR changes the appraisals and meaning of something that is stressing us and weakens negative emotions which in turn increases the likelihood of resilience.

In general, positive emotions can lead to better coping skills, resilience, and overall well-being. Fostering positive emotions is a valuable skill for promoting resilience. With repeated intention and effort to build and strengthen positive emotions through activities such as meditation, relaxation, positive imagery, gratitude, and optimistic thinking, then we are experiencing positive emotions repeatedly and this can be helpful during times of stress. Do not get me wrong, I believe that we should allow negative emotions an opportunity to unfold so that we can deal with them. Just do not become immersed in them to the point where we are thinking thoughts derived from the negative feelings which in turn reinforce the negative feelings. This is a cycle that can lead to prolonged negative feelings, mood swings, or even depression. Instead, focus on what is causing these negative feelings on work on solving the issue in a positive way as possible.

One particularly good study examined how resilience and positive emotions affect how negative emotions are experienced during times of stress. Can positive emotions moderate the effects of stress, how well we recover, and how well we can resist stress? The results supported the notion that higher levels of positive emotions weakened the influence of stress from negative emotions. Also, highly resilient people experience positive emotions even when going through stressful events; they draw on those positive emotions to rebound from negative emotions.

Five Steps to Overcome Negative Thoughts

Self-limiting beliefs are at the core of self-doubt, insecurities, and often a lack of self-control. Self-limiting beliefs can take root when negative suggestions are repeatedly directed toward us. We can start to believe the criticisms, disapproving comments, and fault-finding remarks from others (especially from perceived "authority figures") regardless of whether they are based on truth. At some point, we may internalize these suggestions to the point that they become self-suggestions. We begin to tell ourselves these negative things. With enough repetition, these negative thoughts become automatic. Self-doubt is almost instantaneous and nearly imperceptible.

However, regardless of how the seeds of self-limiting beliefs were planted and allowed to bear the fruit of self-doubt and insecurities, we have the power to change. Through the same mechanisms of self-suggestion, we can plant new seeds of positive beliefs and self-confidence that create new habits that help us instead of hinder us. Now, I don't want to imply that I believe everything is always going to be perfect and through wishful thinking, we will never encounter a setback. Also, I know it's important to be aware of risks and potential consequences for a given set of decisions, but this awareness should lead us to action instead of wallowing in fear. Sometimes it just seems easier for people to beat themselves up rather than to lift themselves. I hear people saying things like "I can't do it" or "I messed up again" or "I'll never be good at that." Some people tend to say these things a lot, but the reason they are saying them is that those types of statements are congruent with their self-limiting beliefs. That's why it may feel a little goofy when we tell ourselves positive affirmations, but if we will push through it, these will eventually replace the negative statements.

The first step that I propose in correcting our negative thoughts and self-doubt is to recognize them when they happen. This is easier said than done. It may be easier to start by paying close attention to our reactions to others and events. We need to set a strong intention to reflect on our reactions as soon as we can after they occur. With practice, we will start to recognize the thoughts and feelings before the reaction occurs. Next, we must take full responsibility for our thoughts, feelings, and behaviors. We should not blame others, circumstances, or events that are going on around us for how we feel and how we behave. This is like saying "I'm not in control, other people and events control me." Do not allow that to happen. We can start to take responsibility by simply saying the words "I am responsible for my thoughts, feelings, and actions at this moment." Another powerful method is to write it down. When we say it or write it down, we should immediately feel a sense of control.

After taking responsibility, we may feel some shame or guilt for our thoughts, feelings, and behaviors. This may be why we were avoiding taking responsibility all along! At this point, we need to forgive ourselves. Self-forgiveness is a foundational step to move forward and learn the lesson. What I mean by "the lesson" is realizing that we could have reacted differently (i.e., exercised more self-control), think about how we want to handle a similar situation in the future, and understand what triggered our reaction so that we can be better tune in to the trigger the next time it happens. After we learn the lesson, we move on. We should not ruminate on the negative aspects or continue to beat ourselves up over the situation. We will now tend to look for the next opportunity to practice and become incrementally better.

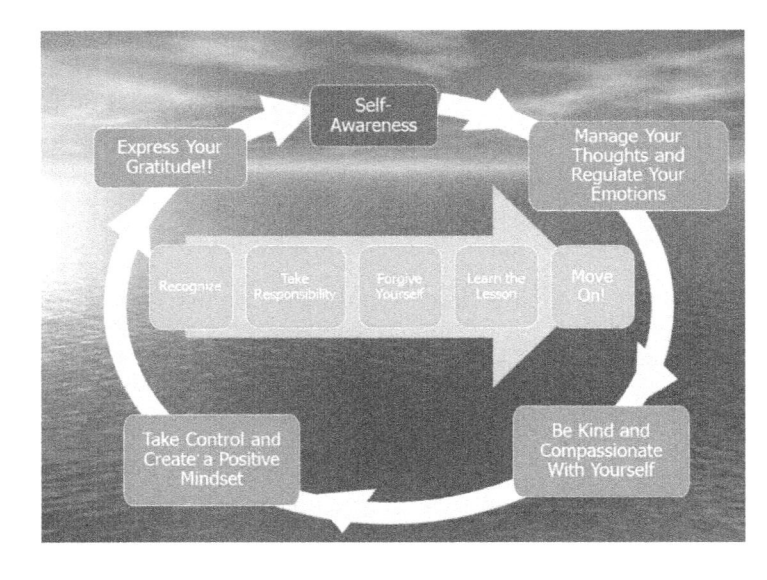

Practicing these steps can create a new cycle of improvement. We gain self-awareness from recognizing and taking responsibility. We can now take control of our thoughts and emotions. Next, we take charge of how we treat ourselves.

We become kinder and more compassionate through self-forgiveness. By seeing the lesson, we establish a more positive mindset. Finally, we should always express our gratitude for the good we have created through this process and we will seek more of the same. We should have an outward expression of our thoughts and beliefs that is more positive. Generally, these outward expressions are smiling, friendliness, happiness, and a desire to help others feel good about themselves. Now, we are getting somewhere.

Resilience

Do you ever find yourself getting caught up in other people's opinions? Too little-too big, too smart-too dumb, too caring-too selfish, too this-too that, and the list goes on. How about taking a moment to appreciate who you are right now and all you have been through to get here? How about appreciating the fact that you are self-aware enough to acknowledge your strengths and weaknesses, keeping your ego in check while having high self-esteem, and striving toward your self-prescribed goals to become better in some way while being grateful for where your path leads you as you persevere to keep striding? I used to worry about what other people thought about me. It was so bad that if I thought someone didn't like me, I felt down for days and I wondered, "Did I do something wrong?" or "What's wrong with me?" It is easy to feel we need everyone's approval and to think we should say the right things, change our behavior for each individual and situation to attain their approval. However, a big problem happens when we lose our identity and can no longer be authentic. We forget who we are. Through self-awareness and some introspection, I believe we can get back to our authentic selves and it doesn't mean we have to become cold, rigid, and snub everyone we meet. Instead, we can be authentic, stay within our values, and not get caught up in worrying about everyone's approval while at the same time be kind, caring, and a good person. Do not let setbacks and failures overshadow your efforts or your ability to pick yourself up when down and take on the next challenge with more experience, wisdom, and compassion.

I wrote my doctoral dissertation on how leaders overcome failure and I have included some of my work in this book. Failure, the quintessential word that simultaneously conjures up images of hopelessness and perseverance, ironically encompasses the possible consequences that can simultaneously exist when a risk is taken or not taken. Failure can beget more failure and lead to a series of disappointing outcomes or imbue profound growth in character and wisdom that serve as the preconditions to success that would have otherwise not been achieved. Experiencing a failure can stymie the greatest of effort or spring forth the will to persevere through a multitude of subsequent setbacks. There is a hypocritical undertone when speaking of failure: it is inevitable and experiencing it can lead to deep learning if reflected on properly, but let's make sure we avoid it all costs because there is an overwhelming expectation of negative consequences. Unfortunately, failure and fault tend to be highly correlated in most households, organizations, and cultures. At some point, we have probably experienced where admitting failure means taking the blame. The idea of fault summons feelings of potential punishment. There is a fear of failure that drives a deeply rooted motivation to evade it, feel high levels of anxiety from it, and take a stance of prevarication when questioned about it.

From their book, The Art and Adventure of Leadership: Understanding Failure, Resilience, and Success, Bennis, Sample, and Asghar inform the reader on the etymology of the word *fail*. They explain that *fail* is derived from the French word *faillir*, which means "to almost do" and faillir is derived in turn from the Latin word *fallere*, which means to deceive or "lead into error." These definitions imply that when people fail, they do not follow through with their intentions, and those who believed that they would be in some way deceived. Therefore, even though the idea of embracing and learning from failure is pervasive in current literature, there can be a sense of shame felt by people who experience a failure, and this emotional response can cause them to suppress their feelings, deflect the responsibility of the failure, neglect to learn from the valuable lessons and thwart the possibility for future success. This always begs the question, how do we overcome this?

Regarding self-regulation, Bandura proposes that through systematic self-observation, a self-diagnostic function can arise where an understanding of how thoughts affect emotional states and motivation can be gained. Specifically, we need to observe our thought patterns, emotional reactions, and behaviors to understand our patterns. These patterns are hiding in broad daylight. If we are not aware of them, then we have not made an effort to do so. Sometimes, others can point them out to us, but we have to receptive to that feedback to allow ourselves to think about it. We must recognize these patterns to correct them. Once we set our intention on recognizing our patterns and doing the work necessary, such as being self-aware, writing about our emotional responses and behaviors, and talking to others we trust, then we will start seeing them. This process of corrective change is critical if we are to overcome a negatively oriented mindset established during the period immediately following any kind of setback.

Resilience is about understanding and correcting our emotional and cognitive after experiencing some kind of event that has affected us negatively. We may develop a self-defeating attitude after experiencing some event in our life such as a conflict or setback. We must employ an act of will to overcome these prevailing attitudes. We must convert our will into actions by planning, purposely creating new behaviors, and controlling our impulses. Resilience is a process over time that involves learning and self-development after adversity. It's about how we think and feel about the issue and what we do about it. It is not always easy for us to gather evidence of a situation objectively and balance the needed optimism with the right dose of a realistic understanding of risks and consequences after experiencing a setback.

When adversity is met with perseverance,
When barriers crumble at the hands of persistence,
When positivity shines a light on the bleak,
When strength is summoned each time you feel weak,
Then no matter the distance and no matter the toll,
Nothing will stop you from reaching your goal.

Bouncing Back

When we bounce back from adversity, conflict, or setback, then we have undergone behavioral changes and have taken action to re-engage ourselves in a way to once again be positive. At this point of the process, the interplay between our emotions and thoughts has led us to overcome being too hard on ourselves and have a sense of empowerment to overcome the situation. Through effort, we can change ourselves. Our beliefs about our capabilities, or self-efficacy, are central to exercising control over a situation and function as important determinants of thoughts, feelings, and behaviors. Believe in yourself! Believe in your abilities, how much effort you will exert toward your goal, and the amount of stress, anxiety, or depression you will experience when taking action to pursue your goals. We must have the intention, commitment, planning, self-appraisal, and (d) self-reflection. Once we make a decision, we set the wheels in motion. Once we have become convinced that we have what it takes to succeed, we will persevere in the face of adversity, and through determination, we will overcome.

From my research on overcoming failure and bouncing back, I learned several things. I interviewed 10 business leaders and they opened up to me about their experiences. The qualitative research led me to find themes across all participants. First, how the respondents viewed and ascribed the cause or causes of their setbacks did not have an effect on their ability to overcome the setback. In other words, some people gave external factors as the cause of their failure while others presented internal causes, but all followed somewhat similar paths along their journey to overcome their failures. Therefore, following a negative event, it may not be important to focus on the causes, at least right away, but instead concentrate on how the person has been impacted.

Second, it was encouraging to hear the leaders open up and express how they felt following their negative event. I expected that even though these leaders showed resilience in their ability to bounce back, they still experienced negative feelings and thoughts after their failure, but I wasn't sure how they would respond because there can be an expectation to appear strong and in control at all times. From this, it seems that whether or not someone can cope, express resilience, and bounce back cannot be predicted solely based on their initial reactions.

Third, the coping and adaptive mechanisms expressed by them varied, but social support was the characteristic most often mentioned. In most cases, social support appeared to have initiated the internal shift from a negative viewpoint to one comprised of optimism, determination, goal setting, planning, and overall positive outlook. Could these people who experienced a failure in their business or workplace have arrived to a more resilient state on their own? Perhaps, but because they specifically mentioned social support, it demonstrated a significant importance it had for them. The implication is that people should receive this support as quickly as possible. But, will a person know or be willing to seek social support following a setback? Maybe not, but people such as family and friends should be aware of the importance of social support, and it would benefit people to know that coaching and counseling could be a beneficial way to help get them back on track. This social support may also be an important factor for regulating their emotions and changing the meaning of the event to one of a more positive outlook. As an example, instead of continuing to be sad or angry because of the event, they are now happy the event happened because something more interesting can be pursued.

Fourth, for the leaders interviewed, bouncing back was about translating positive thoughts and feelings into affirming beliefs and actions. These actions included helping others or volunteering in some way, self-improvement activities such as working on a new degree, and making positive changes such as opening a new business. Therefore, if someone has suffered a setback, whether or not action has been taken by the individual may be an indicator of where they are in the process of bouncing back. Also, it may be important to recognize the right time to encourage behaviors that are action oriented. If we attempt to inspire someone to take action before they are ready, will it have an undesirable effect? This question can't be answered based on my research, but the study suggests that positive behaviors naturally follow positive feelings and thoughts.

Last, the interviewees expressed what they learned from their experience and in general, they were more focused on being better prepared and risk management for what could go wrong that could lead to another failure. This suggests that regardless of the individual perceptions of the cause or causes of their setback, they are taking it upon themselves to avert a future setback by watching for the indicators that alert them to an impending negative event and managing the risks associated with them. Additionally, leadership styles appeared to have changed such that these leaders exhibit more compassion toward their employees and encourage participation. This all implies a lot of effort, change, and motivation to overcome a setback or failure from the negative feelings and thoughts to taking action.

I think a lot about "effort." There are some things for which I don't want to put forth much effort and for others, I feel like I could move a mountain. For me, it comes down to 3 P's: Purpose, Passion, and a Plan. My purpose is the "why?" and a goal is meaningless without it. We may have an internal goal that is not in alignment with an external goal and that's why we don't make progress. If so, we need to check our purpose. Passion is almost indescribable and is a feeling that fuels my energy. A plan is the "how" and while there can be different ways to get where we are going, pick the best for you and remember to remain adaptable.

For me, change seems to follow the law of increasing returns. According to Harvard Business Review, "Increasing returns are the tendency for that which is ahead to get further ahead, for that which loses advantage to lose further advantage. They are mechanisms of positive feedback...." In other words, the greater the effort, then the greater the return which brings forth more effort. The problem for me is in the beginning when I think I am putting in a lot of effort, but I'm not and I'm not getting the return that I'm expecting. It can be disheartening. This is because relatively speaking I am putting in more, but on an absolute scale, I have much more to give and so it follows that the true reward is out there waiting on me to decide how badly I want it and to come to get it. So, if you are not strong out of the gates, then don't expect to get what you want until you dig in and put forth the effort needed. If it is worth it, you'll find a way and the rewards will be proportional to what you give. Believe in yourself, keep going, dig deep, and allow the wonderful things that will surely come your way.

I sometimes wonder what exactly motivation is and from where it is derived. I've read and studied several different motivational theories from Maslow to McClelland's needs, Hertzberg's Two-Factor, along with Equity, Expectancy, Goal-Setting and others. For me, if I am unmotivated to do something, then it means I am either content with my current state or lacking the drive to take action. If I am not content with my current state, then I probably want to change it and I'm ready to do something about it. There is some reason or a combination of reasons that may come from internal or external environmental forces that motivate me. I will most likely decide to take some action to make the change a reality. If at this point I decide not to take action, then I will have to deal with negative feelings or other undesirable consequences. Based on all this, I have come up with a definition for motivation that works for me: Behavior is influenced by some combination of intrinsic and/or extrinsic factors in an attempt to achieve a desired state or goal, while simultaneously attempting to avoid potential negative consequences derived from within or outside of my control. Do you have your definition?

It is important to understand that an attitude we are experiencing now can probably be traced back to our prior thoughts. When we visualize a negative outcome, we may experience negative emotions and we may have a fear of the imagined consequences that could occur as a result of the anticipated negative outcome. But, by thinking and visualizing a positive outcome thinking and visualizing a positive outcome that is both believable and attainable, we will most likely experience positive emotions. It is about our expectations. If we believe and expect good things to happen, then our attitude, behavior, and actions will support the expectations. We will be open to the changes that will positively affect our lives and the lives of others. Positive thinking does not mean that you keep your head in the sand and ignore life's less pleasant situations. Positive thinking just means that you approach unpleasantness more positively and productively. You think the best is going to happen, not the worst.

Summary

These are characteristics that are important to me. GRIP exemplifies the habits that I want to create and maintain. Think of it this way: Gratitude creates a state of mind that prepares us to take Responsibility; we are more balanced, grounded, receptive, and open. Taking Responsibility for what is in your control opens the door to Improvement. The continuous effort for Improvement and succeeding leads to Positivity. This cycles back to give you more for which to be grateful. I strive daily to practice these characteristics and further ingrain them into my character and personality. Do I make mistakes? Of course. Do I fall short? Absolutely, but I remember to get a GRIP. Check out this simple and straightforward exercise. No matter what you are grappling with, you can:

1. For every problem or struggle, find one thing for which to be grateful.

2. What about this issue can you accept responsibility?

3. What would you improve and how are you going to do it? Develop a goal, strategy, or plan.

4. What positive outcome can you envision by accomplishing this goal?

Remember, there is a difference between knowing the path and walking the path; the path that we walk is the path that we choose.

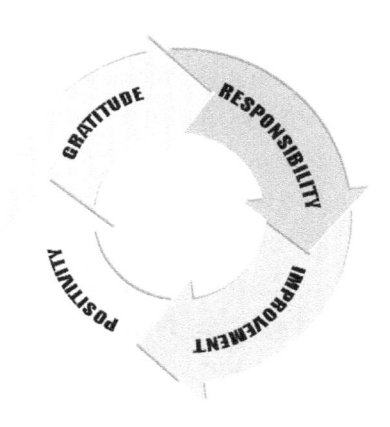

I leave you with my 10 If's:

1. If you can imagine a better life for yourself and you want it badly enough, then go for it.

2. If you constantly compare yourself to others, then you will always find someone better than you at something and you will never feel good enough.

3. If you only focus on your mistakes and failures, then you will always feel like a mistake and a failure.

4. If you always see the worst in others, then you probably always see the worst in yourself.

5. If you are constantly blaming others for what's wrong in your life, then you're not taking responsibility for what you can change.

6. If you forgive yourself for your shortcomings, then you will find it easier to forgive others for theirs.

7. If there is an area in your life that you want to improve, then get started and seek all the help you need.

8. If you find yourself in an unhealthy environment, then it's your responsibility to remove yourself from it.

9. If you can find peace in the moment, then there will always be moments when you can find peace.

10. If you can lift someone, then do it because they are probably beating themselves up over something that is truly insignificant.

I hope that I have helped you in some way and when life seems to be slipping through your fingers, remember to get a GRIP.

About the Author

Richard Leo Hunt, EdD has three degrees from Western Kentucky University: BS in Chemistry, MS in Engineering Technology Management, and EdD in Organizational Leadership. Richard is a veteran of the US Army and served on active duty from 1989 – 1995. He has owned a business, taught at the collegiate level, done public speaking, and has held a quality management role in various industries. Richard is also an actor with several credits to his name.

Questions? Concerns? Need personal coaching?

Richard Leo Hunt
Richardleohunt.com
richardleohunt@gmail.com

Richard Leo Hunt ©
All rights reserved.

Made in the USA
Monee, IL
15 May 2021